THE BOOK OF STARS

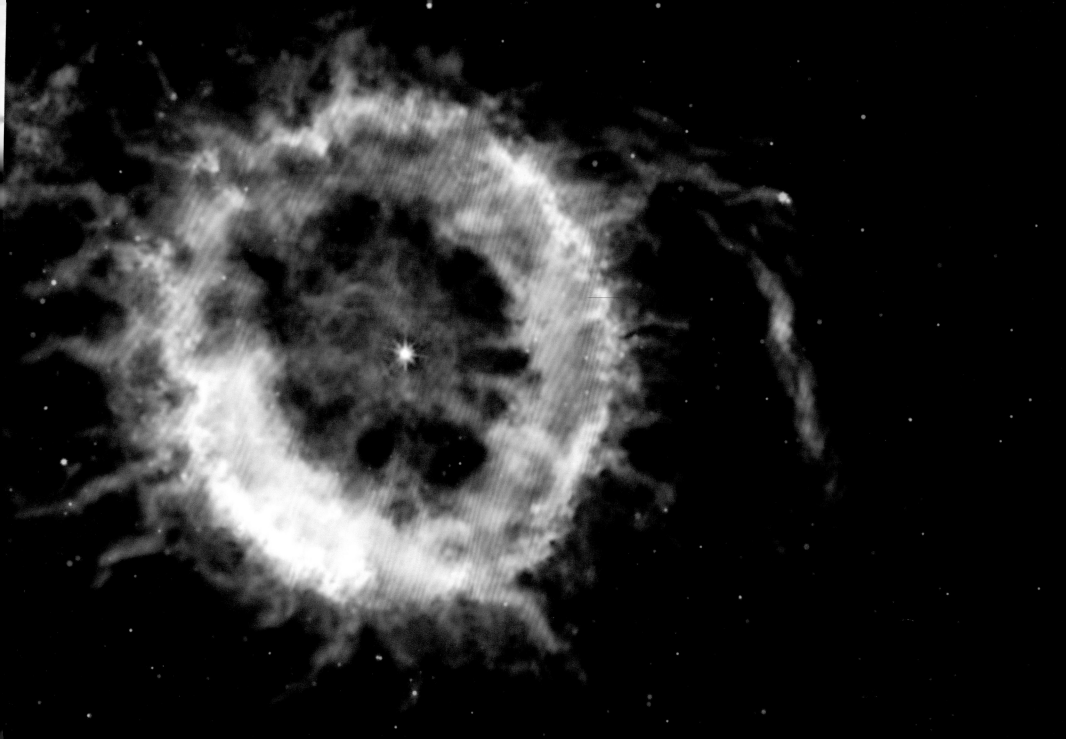

THE BOOK OF STARS

AUTHOR: Clint Twist
ILLUSTRATOR: Kuo Kang Chen
ART EDITOR: Duncan Brown
EDITOR: Elise See Tai
ART DIRECTOR: Miranda Kennedy
EDITORIAL MANAGER: Ruth Hooper
PRODUCTION DIRECTOR: Clive Sparling

Created by Pinwheel
A Division of Alligator Books Ltd
Winchester House
259–269 Old Marylebone Road
London NW1 5XJ, UK
www.pinwheel.co.uk

This edition produced in 2007 for Scholastic Inc.
Published by Tangerine Press, an imprint of Scholastic Inc.,
557 Broadway; New York, NY 10012

ISBN-10: 0-545-05471-0
ISBN-13: 978-0-545-05471-3

9 8 7 6 5 4 3 2 1

Printed in Malaysia

CONTENTS

THE SUN

The Sun shines brightly in space. Heat and light from the Sun make Earth a good place to live. The Sun is a star—the nearest star to Earth. It is one of billions of stars in the universe. A star is a very large ball of gas. Heat and light are produced by nuclear energy at the center of the star. All stars have the same basic structure, but there are many differences in their size and appearance. The Sun is a fairly small star with a yellowish color. It is classified as a *yellow dwarf star*.

MYTHS AND LEGENDS

Ancient Greek astronomers believed that the Earth was at the center of the universe. They believed that a series of transparent crystal spheres surrounded the Earth and contained the Sun, Moon, planets, and stars. According to Greek astronomers, the seventh and outermost crystal sphere held the stars.

THE SUN

FACTS AND FIGURES

DIAMETER: 870,000 miles
MASS: about 300,000 times the mass of Earth
CORE TEMPERATURE: 27 million °F
SURFACE TEMPERATURE: 10,800°F
DISTANCE FROM EARTH: 93 million miles

RED DWARF

Most stars produce less light and heat than the Sun. Many of these stars are classified as *red dwarfs*. These are stars that are too small to have much nuclear energy. Instead of shining hot and bright, red dwarfs have a surface temperature of about 6,000°F and glow with a dim red light. Red dwarfs cannot be seen from Earth with the unaided eye. They produce about a million times less light than the Sun, and can be seen with special telescopes.

MYTHS AND LEGENDS

Another type of star, the *brown dwarf*, may be the answer to one of the biggest problems in science. The problem is that there are not enough stars to account for the mass of the universe. About 80 percent of the mass appears to be "missing." Some scientists believe that the "missing" mass is contained in trillions of brown dwarfs, which are even smaller and dimmer than red dwarfs.

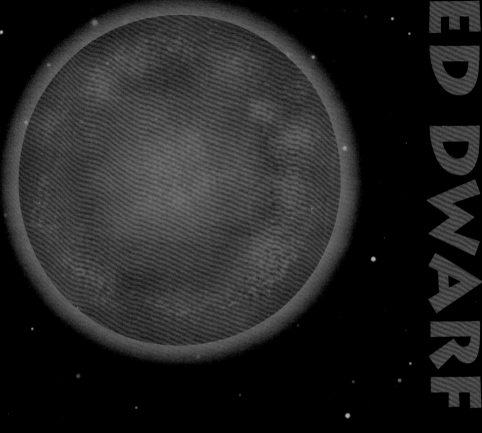

RED DWARF

LOOKING CLOSER

The second nearest star to the Earth is the red dwarf *Proxima Centauri*, which is more than 280,000 times farther away than the Sun.

Giant Star

Stars that are more than 10 times the size of the Sun are known as *giants*. The biggest stars are called *supergiants*. Stars that are hotter and brighter than the Sun are classified as *white stars* because they shine with a bluish-white light. The star *Rigel* is a white supergiant about 30 times larger than the Sun. Rigel is in the constellation *Orion* and is a lot bigger, brighter, and hotter than the Sun. Stars like Rigel burn very hotly and quickly. After a few million years, they explode with a brief, bright burst of light. This explosion is called a *supernova*.

Myths and Legends

In 1054, Chinese astronomers noted a new star that shone brightly for a time and then disappeared. In 1731, a European astronomer discovered the *Crab Nebula*—a glowing cloud in the constellation *Taurus*. Modern astronomers are now certain that the Crab Nebula is the remains of the supernova explosion first observed in China.

LOOKING CLOSER

Without supernovas, there would not only be no life on Earth, there would be no Earth. Nearly all chemical elements, including carbon, can only be made and distributed by supernova explosions. Many of the rocks on Earth and all plants and animals contain carbon.

GIANT STAR

MYTHS AND LEGENDS

There are many myths about the end of the world. The Vikings believed it would end with a great battle called *Ragnarok*. The ancient Iranians believed the world would be washed clean by a river of molten metal. In fact, however, the world will probably end about 5 million years from now, when the Sun expands to become a red giant.

LOOKING CLOSER

Stars shine by converting mass into energy. The Sun has been shining for about 4.5 billion years. It "burns" about 4 million tons of mass every second. Even at this rate, the Sun has more than enough mass to continue shining for at least another 4.5 billion years.

DYING STAR

DOUBLE STAR

To the unaided eye, stars look like tiny lights in the night sky. A small telescope allows many more stars to be seen and makes it easier to see color differences, but the stars still look like points of light. With a powerful telescope, it is possible to see that some stars are not actually single points of light. These stars are two separate points of light that are very close together. They are known as *double stars*. Sirius, the brightest star visible from Earth, is a double star. A white dwarf, called *Sirius B*, orbits very closely around a much larger and brighter white star, called *Sirius A*.

MYTHS AND LEGENDS

The ancient Egyptians believed that Sirius had a powerful influence over events on Earth because it is the brightest star in the night sky. They timed their calendar to begin on the night that Sirius first appeared each year.

LOOKING CLOSER

There are many double, triple, and even quadruple stars. Proxima Centauri, a red dwarf, is actually part of a triple star. This triple star is usually known by the name of the brightest of the three stars—*Alpha Centauri*.

DOUBLE STAR

Star Cluster

Stars are born inside large, swirling clouds of gas and dust called *nebulae*. Like the Sun, most stars are born with no close neighbors, unless they are very close, as in a double star. Sometimes, however, a number of stars are born close together around the same time to form a *star cluster*. Actual star clusters, with the stars close together, are very rare. Many of the "clusters" that are seen with the unaided eye are stars that are actually far apart and just look close together. The most famous star cluster is the *Pleiades*, often known as the *Seven Sisters* because of the seven brightest stars in the cluster.

Myths and Legends

According to the Iroquois people of North America, the Pleiades were seven bad children who had been told to stop dancing. They danced away until they danced themselves into the sky.

Looking Closer

Distances in the universe are measured in *light years*. This is the distance light travels in a year—about 5.8 trillion miles. The distance between the Sun and Proxima Centauri is 4.25 light years. The Pleiades are about 1,400 light years away. The 400 or so stars in the cluster are all grouped within 50 light years of each other.

Galaxy

The Sun, along with all the other stars that can be seen at night, is part of the galaxy called the *Milky Way*. A galaxy is a vast "star city" that contains billions of stars. Some galaxies are egg-shaped, some are disc-shaped, some are spirals, and some have an irregular shape. Our Milky Way galaxy is a spiral galaxy with the stars grouped at the center and along a series of "arms" that spiral outward. The Sun is located on one of these arms, about halfway between the center and the outer edges of the galaxy.

Myths and Legends

In the American Southwest, the Mescalero Apache had their own name for the Milky Way—the *Scattered Seeds*. They believed that the stars had been spilled from a container of seeds carried by one of their war gods.

LOOKING CLOSER

The Milky Way Galaxy is about 75,000 light years in diameter. It contains approximately 200 billion stars, including the Sun. The Sun is located on a spiral arm called the *Orion Arm*, which is also known as the *Local Arm*. Other spiral arms are named *Perseus Arm*, *Sagittarius Arm*, and *Scutum-Crux Arm*.

GALAXY

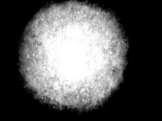

Elliptical Galaxy

Barred Spiral Galaxy

Irregular Galaxy

Spiral Galaxy

UNIVERSE

Beyond the Milky Way galaxy, there is nothing in any direction but thousands of light years of empty space. The nearest galaxy to our own is about 200,000 light years away. This is how the universe looks—clusters of matter in the form of galaxies separated by huge amounts of space. The view is always the same, even with the most powerful telescopes—bright galaxies in the dark emptiness of space. The universe stretches endlessly in all directions.

MYTHS AND LEGENDS

There is a widespread belief that sometime in the future human beings will travel between distant planets and stars—perhaps in a few hundred years or so. Unfortunately, such travel is impossible according to all the laws of science that we have discovered so far. The only hope for space travel is for a scientist to discover an entirely new branch of science.

LOOKING CLOSER

The most powerful telescopes can only show galaxies that are about 13.5 billion light years away. It is impossible to know the size of the universe, because it is always expanding.

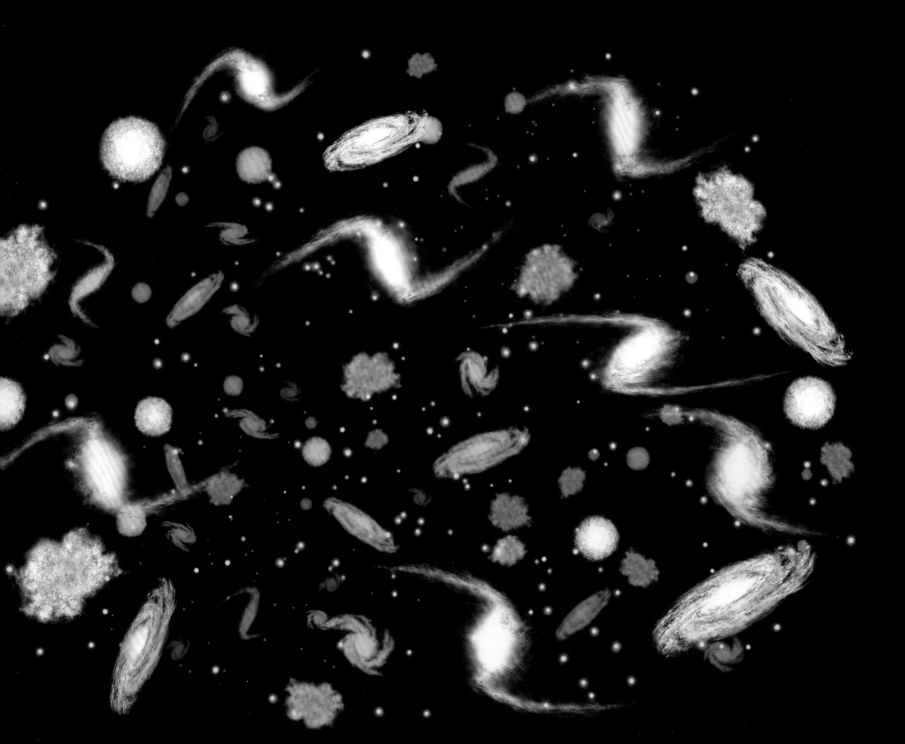

STAR SHAPES

People see recognizable shapes in natural features, and stars are no exception. By joining together the brighter stars with lines, ancient people were able to "see" a variety of shapes in the night sky. Such arrangements of stars are known as *constellations*. Some constellations and their stories have been passed down through the ages. Constellations are still used today as a way to map the night sky.

CENTAURUS (THE CENTAUR)

According to ancient Greek legend, a centaur was half human and half horse. The Centaurus constellation takes the shape of a centaur. Proxima Centauri, the red dwarf, is situated near the star Alpha Centauri in the front hooves. The Crux (cross) constellation appears close to Centaurus.

Big Dipper

URSA MAJOR (THE GREAT BEAR)

Legend says that a beautiful Greek girl was changed into a bear by a jealous goddess. The seven stars that form Ursa Major's tail and part of the body make the constellation known as the the *Big Dipper*.

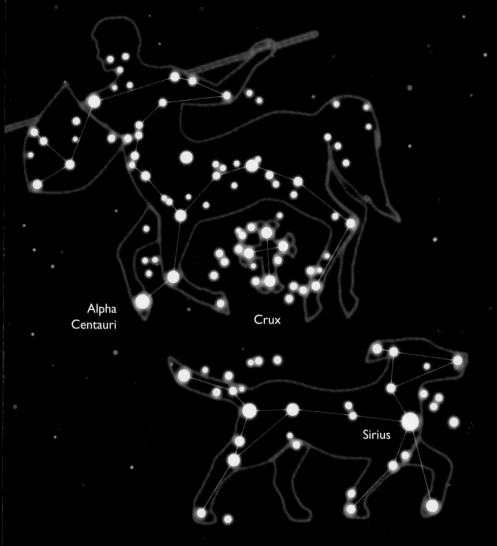

Alpha Centauri

Crux

Sirius

Rigel

CANIS MAJOR (THE GREAT DOG)

Canis Major is one of two "star dogs" that appear close to Orion the Hunter. The very bright star Sirius, also known as the *Dog Star*, is located in the neck.

ORION (THE HUNTER)

Orion was a Greek hero remembered forever in the stars by the gods. The easiest stars to see are the three in Orion's belt. Rigel, a supergiant star, is located in the hunter's raised foot.

NIGHT SKIES

The night sky is never exactly the same two nights in a row. The stars appear to move very slowly across the sky. The many different constellations are seen according to an annual cycle. The apparent movement of the stars is a result of Earth's year-long orbit of the Sun. As Earth moves through space, the view of the stars changes accordingly.

STAR VIEWING

What is seen when looking up on a cloudless night depends on three things—the location on Earth in terms of longitude (position north or south of the Equator), the time of year, and the time of night. Longitude determines what part of the whole night sky can be seen. A person near the Equator will have a very different view than someone near the Poles. The time of year determines which constellations are visible from Earth according to the annual cycle. The time of night determines the exact position of the stars.

NORTHERN HEMISPHERE SUMMER

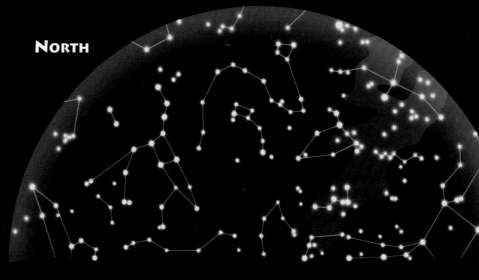

NORTH

West   Ea

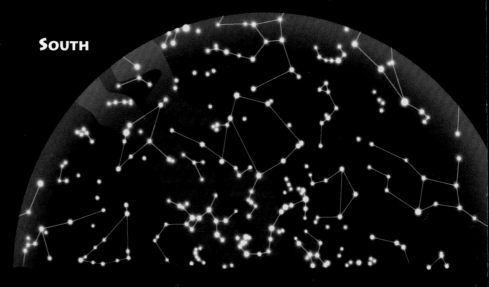

SOUTH

East   We

LIFE CYCLE

A medium-sized star like the Sun has a life cycle that lasts between eight and 12 billion years.

Deep inside a thick, dusty nebula, a new star flares into life. Material left over from the star-making process may form planets that orbit the star, just as Earth orbits the Sun.

For nearly all of its long, long life, the star "burns" smoothly and steadily with a bright yellow light. At the core of the star, vast amounts of energy are produced by the element hydrogen being converted into the element helium.

After billions of years, the star runs out of hydrogen and begins converting helium instead. The star gradually swells to more than 200 times larger than it was and becomes a red giant with a surface temperature of only about 5,400°F.

The star then s quantities of n What remains very hot, whit expanding bul

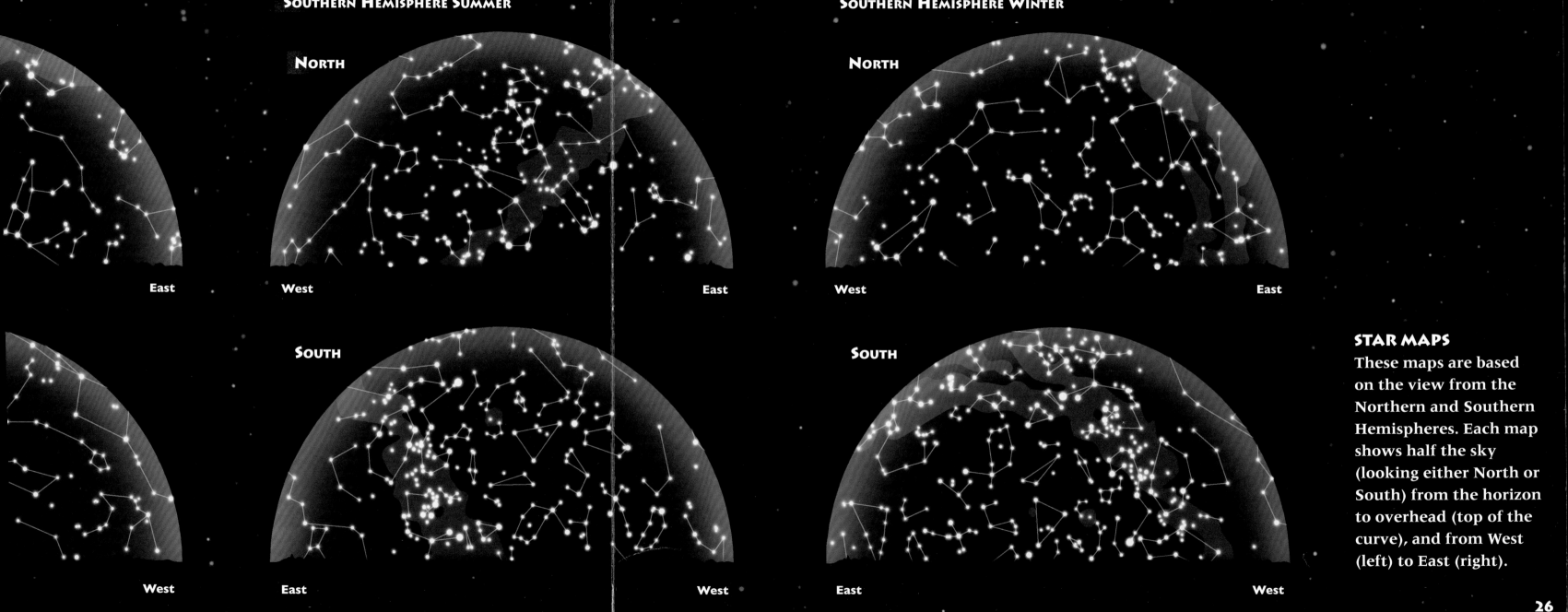

NORTH

East

West

East

NORTH

West

East

SOUTH

West

East

SOUTH

West

West

East

East

West

STAR MAPS

These maps are based on the view from the Northern and Southern Hemispheres. Each map shows half the sky (looking either North or South) from the horizon to overhead (top of the curve), and from West (left) to East (right).

Glossary

CONSTELLATION
A visible grouping of stars that appear to form a recognizable shape.

ELEMENT
One of the 92 basic chemical substances that occur naturally on Earth.

GALAXY
A grouping of about one billion stars.

LIGHT YEAR
The distance a beam of light travels in one year—about 5.8 trillion miles.

MILKY WAY
A band of stars in the night sky; the galaxy in which the Sun is located.

NEBULA
A cloud of gases and dust drifting in space.

ORBIT
To travel through space around a planet or star; the path through space made by an orbiting object.

RED DWARF
Small, dim star without enough mass to shine hotly and brightly.

RED GIANT
A star toward the end of its life cycle, when it cools and expands greatly in size.

SIRIUS
The brightest star in the sky, also known as the *Dog Star*.

STAR
A huge, spinning ball of hot gas in space with a maximum size of more than 6 million miles in diameter.

SUN
The nearest star to Earth, and the center of the solar system.

SUPERNOVA
An enormously bright explosion that happens when a supergiant star dies.

TELESCOPE
A device that gives a clearer view of something a long way away. Most telescopes use lenses and curved mirrors to magnify distant objects.

WHITE DWARF
A small, hot star that remains after the collapse of the red giant stage of a star's life cycle.

INDEX